First published in Great Britain 2018 by Farshore
This edition published in Great Britain 2024 by Farshore
An imprint of HarperCollins*Publishers*
1 London Bridge Street, London SE1 9GF
www.farshore.co.uk

HarperCollins*Publishers*
Macken House, 39/40 Mayor Street Upper,
Dublin 1, D01 C9W8, Ireland

ISBN 978 1 4052 9135 4
Printed in Malaysia
023

A CIP catalogue record for this title is available from the British Library.

Stay safe online. Farshore is not responsible for content hosted by third parties.

This book is produced from independently certified FSC™ paper
to ensure responsible forest management.

For more information visit: www.harpercollins.co.uk/green

HOW TO SOLVE

THE  CUBE

"If you are curious, you'll find the puzzles around you. If you are determined, you will solve them."

- Ernő Rubik

CONTENTS

THE RUBIK'S FAMILY

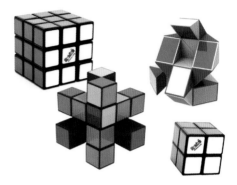

HOW TO SOLVE THE CUBE

HISTORY OF THE RUBIK'S CUBE

Ernő Rubik was born in Budapest, Hungary in 1944, the son of Magdolna Szántó, a poet, and Ernő Rubik Sr, an aircraft engineer and designer of gliders. As a child Rubik was inspired by his father's ability to solve complex problems; he studied at the Budapest University of Technology and eventually became a professor of architecture.

1944
Ernő Rubik is born in Budapest, Hungary.

1974
Rubik creates the first working prototypes of the Cube.

1975
Rubik patents the 'Magic Cube'.

Magic Cubes are
constructed by hand at
Politechnika

The first working prototype
of the Magic Cube

The puzzle that would eventually become known as the Rubik's Cube was
invented in 1974. The young professor was thinking about ways to inspire
his own students. "In my teaching, I enjoyed creating models to clearly
communicate my thoughts," he says.

The first Cube, handmade by Rubik out of blocks of wood and elastic bands,
was the kind of magical object – one that could be twisted and turned
without, somehow, falling apart – that he hoped would get his pupils thinking
about new ways of making things.

"Once I completed the Cube and demonstrated it to my students, I realised it
was nearly impossible to put down," Rubik says. He had also realised that the
Cube could become a puzzle; by adding coloured stickers to the individual
Cubes, it became a fascinating challenge to scramble and unscramble it.

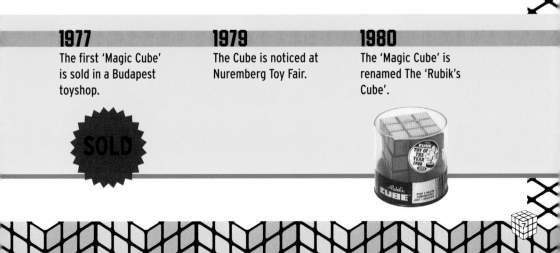

1977
The first 'Magic Cube'
is sold in a Budapest
toyshop.

SOLD

1979
The Cube is noticed at
Nuremberg Toy Fair.

1980
The 'Magic Cube' is
renamed The 'Rubik's
Cube'.

It took Rubik over a month to work out how to solve it. "It was a code I myself had invented! Yet I could not read it," he recalls. Once he had cracked that code, however, the potential of the Cube started to become clear. He patented it in 1975 and started to look for ways to put his magical idea into production.

The first 'Magic Cubes', as they were known, were made in Hungary by a small company called Politechnika, and went on sale in 1977.
At the time, Hungary was still a Communist state with a very tightly-controlled economy, and despite the initial success of the puzzle, this made it very hard to sell internationally. But the Cube nevertheless found its way abroad.

Mathematicians were enchanted by it, and would take it to international conferences to share with their foreign colleagues; and in 1979, a businessman called Tibor Laczi bought one from a waiter in a cafe and decided to take it to the Nuremberg Toy Fair.

1982
The first annual International Rubik's Championships are held.

1990
Professor Rubik becomes President of the Hungarian Engineering Academy.

1995
Diamond Cutters Int. creates the 'Masterpiece Cube'.

The Cube was eventually snapped up by an American company called Ideal Toys, who began to mass produce and sell it in huge quantities. In 1980 and 1981 it was Toy of the Year. By 1982, a staggering 100 million Cubes had been sold. By the mid-1980s, one fifth of the world's population had played with one. It is now the best selling toy of all time.

The impact of the Cube was not just financial. The Cube is a permanent exhibit in the Museum of Modern Art in New York, and has its own entry in the Oxford English Dictionary. Artists used it to create new artworks, in a style called 'Rubik's Cubism'. And it has continued to inspire generations of makers and puzzlers to create their own remarkable objects. The largest working Rubik's Cube is three metres tall and weighs half a ton; the smallest is only ten millimetres tall, but works perfectly.

Engineers have built robots to solve the Cube in the blink of an eye; mathematicians have probed into the complex maths behind it to discover 'God's Number', the maximum number of movements required to solve any scramble. It has inspired a sport – speed-cubing – in which amazing feats of cleverness and dexterity are now commonplace. The Cube has even been into space!

Now you too can learn to crack the world's favourite puzzle! Who knows where it might take you?

2005
The Cube celebrates its 25th Anniversary since launch with a special edition pack.

2007
Professor Rubik awards prizes at the World Championships in Budapest.

2024
The Cube celebrates its 50th anniversary since invention!

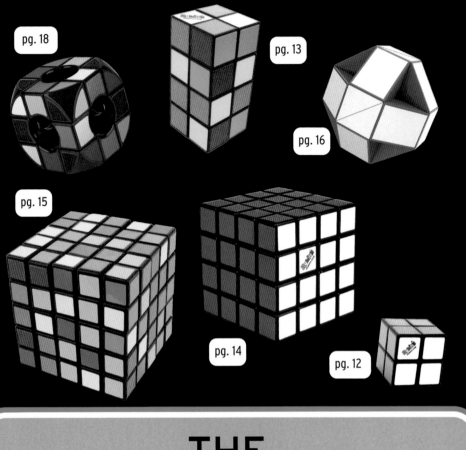

pg. 18

pg. 13

pg. 16

pg. 15

pg. 14

pg. 12

THE
RUBIK'S
FAMILY

The Cube is the best known puzzle in the world – but it was only the first in a line of fiendish challenges ...

THE 3x3x3 CUBE

THE CLASSIC RUBIK'S Cube is a 3x3x3 cube, made of 26 individual cubes (called **cubies**).

When first designed, the colours on each cubie were simple coloured stickers – an easy way to cheat was simply to peel them off and reapply them so that the Cube was 'solved'. The 21st century version uses hard plastic panels glued to the surface, so you'll have to do it the hard way!

INVENTED: By Ernö Rubik, in 1974
SALES: Over 450 million Rubik's Cubes have been sold since it first went on sale. If you were to lay them end to end, these Cubes would stretch the whole length of the Great Wall of China!

THE 2x2x2 CUBE (MINI)

THE 2X2X2 CUBE (Mini Cube) has only eight cubies, but is still a challenge to solve. Unlike the 3x3x3 Cube, all the cubies can move around – there are no centre pieces.

Even this smaller Cube has over 3.6 million different scrambles! Solving it by randomly turning and twisting the Cube could easily take you weeks – and that's if you didn't stop to sleep or eat. Luckily, a little logic will do the job instead (all the techniques you will learn in this book will work on the 2x2x2 Cube).

INVENTED: By Ernö Rubik
RECORDS: The fastest recorded times for solving the 2x2x2 Cube are under a second! The Chinese speed-cuber Guanbo Wang holds the world record for fastest single solve with an amazing 0.47 seconds.

THE TOWER

AS A FASCINATING twist on the Rubik's Cube, there are puzzles which aren't cube-shaped but cuboid. The 2x2x4 'Rubik's Tower' variation can take on some odd shapes while you're solving it, as longer edges are rotated around shorter ones.

DID YOU KNOW: As well as the official 2x2x4 Rubik's Tower there are a whole range of non-cube-shaped puzzles invented by a variety of different puzzle-makers over the years, including 2x2x3, 2x2x5, and even longer ones. There's even a 2x2x13 version!

THE 4X4X4 CUBE (MASTER)

FOR AN EVEN greater challenge, more cubies can be added! The 4x4x4 'Rubik's Revenge' puzzle has **7.4 quattuordecillion** possible scrambles. 1 quattuordecillion is a one with 45 zeroes after it.

Unlike the 3x3x3 Cube, all the centre pieces can move, creating an extra level of difficulty.

Rubik's Revenge was invented by Péter Sebestény in 1980 and works in a quite different way to the original Cube – an internal sphere allows all the different layers to pivot smoothly.

BIGGER CUBES: Even bigger cubes have been created by puzzle fans, including one monster cube which is 22x22x22!

SOLVING: One method to solve the 4x4x4 Cube involves first grouping the centre and edge pieces of each colour together; the Cube can then be solved using the method for the 3x3x3 Cube.

THE 5x5x5 CUBE (PROFESSOR)

THE 5X5X5 CUBE invented in 1981 by Udo Krell is the largest that Rubik's produce. The number of possible ways to scramble the 5x5x5 Cube is a mind-bogglingly huge number that comes close to the number of atoms in the observable universe; nevertheless, the world record for solving it is less than 35 seconds.

RUBIK'S SNAKE

RUBIK'S SNAKE IS another of Ernő Rubik's magical creations, an arrangement of triangular prisms connected by cunning spring-loaded bolts, which allow them to twist without coming apart.

The Snake can be transformed into a variety of geometrical shapes – or even a dog!

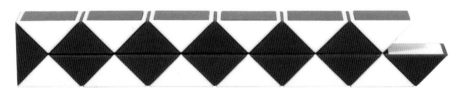

Switchback

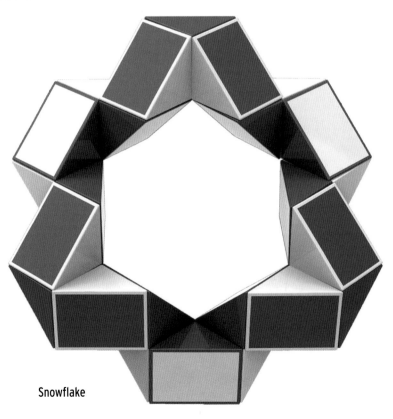

Snowflake

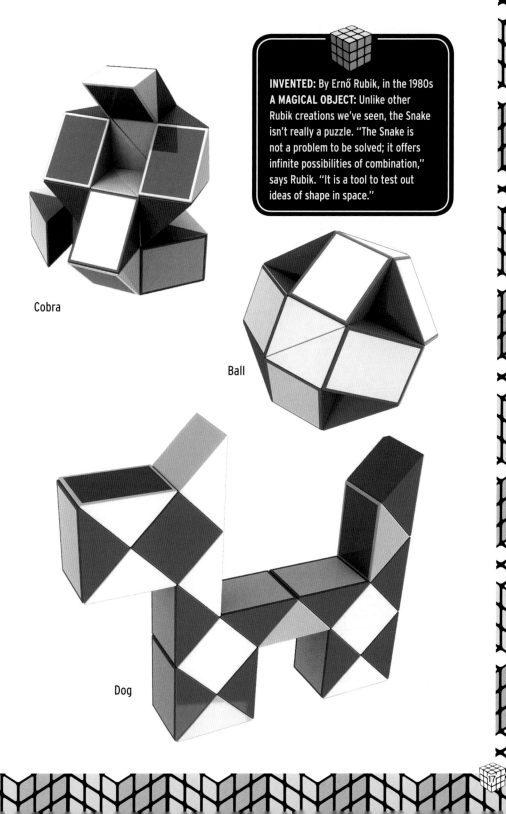

Cobra

Ball

Dog

RUBIK'S MAGIC

RUBIK'S MAGIC, invented by Ernö Rubik in 1985, was a puzzle made up of eight tiles connected to each other by wires so that they could be folded and shuffled into different configurations. The object was to create the linked-rings image shown to the right, but there were many other challenges to master such as creating three-dimensional shapes like stars, chains, boxes and even houses!

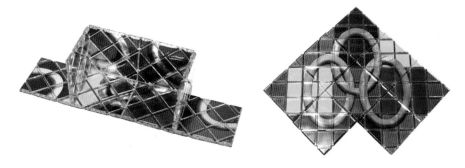

RUBIK'S VOID

RUBIK'S VOID was a variation on the classic Cube created by speed-cubing champion Katsuhiko Okamoto, in which the centre pieces were replaced by holes which went through the entire puzzle.

As well as the appeal of the mysterious mechanism – the original Cube pivoted around a central core, which was entirely removed in the Void – it was harder to solve. With no fixed centre pieces there was no immediately obvious way to tell which face was supposed to be which colour.

HOW TO
SOLVE

THE RUBIK'S CUBE

GET TO KNOW YOUR CUBE

Before we begin, we need to learn some terminology. It's really important to get to know what the parts of your Rubik's Cube are called so that you can follow these instructions!

Corner pieces

Edge pieces

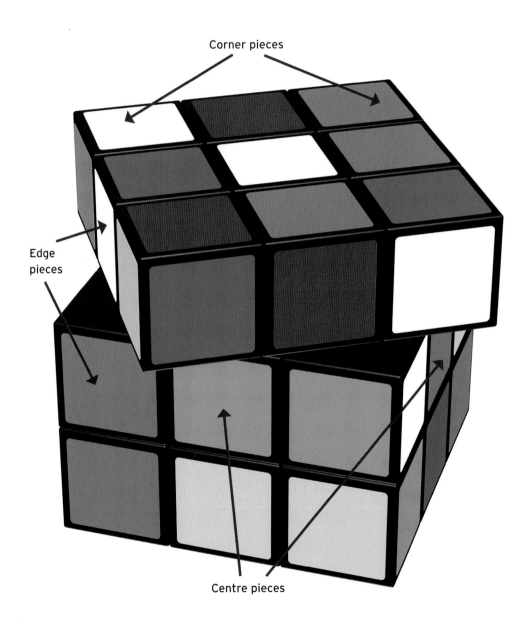

Centre pieces

CUBIES

A standard 3x3x3 Rubik's Cube is made up of 26 smaller cubes, called **cubies**. (There is no cube in the centre!) It's possible for the cubies to become detached from the Cube if you apply some force, but they can easily be snapped back into place. Just make sure that they go back in the correct place, as mixing them up can make the Cube unsolvable.

CENTRE PIECES

There's one in the middle of each face, so 6 in total, one of each colour. The centre pieces never move – so the blue face is the face with a blue centre piece, and so on. While solving the Cube, you will often be using the centre pieces to tell you which face is which.

The 6 centre pieces:

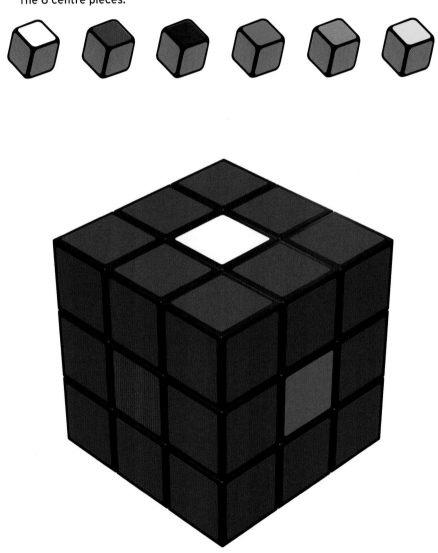

EDGE PIECES

There are 12 of these – one in the middle of each edge. Each one shows two different colours, and joins the two corresponding faces together. When in the right positions they make a cross-shape with the centre piece.

The 12 edge pieces:

CORNER PIECES

There are 8 of these, one at each corner. Each corner piece shows three different colours.

The 8 corner pieces:

NO TWO CUBIES ARE THE SAME

There are nine cubies with at least one white face:

1 centre piece:	4 edge pieces:	4 corner pieces:
white only	white/orange	white/orange/blue
	white/blue	white/orange/green
	white/green	white/green/red
	white/red	white/red/blue

To solve the Cube we need to move all the edge and corner pieces to the unique positions – or '**slots**' – they belong in, so the white/orange/blue corner piece needs to go where the white, orange and blue corners meet, the red/green edge piece needs to go where the red and green faces meet, and so on. There is only one correct **position** for each cubie – none are interchangeable. There is also only one correct **orientation** for each cubie – this means they have to be facing the correct way and not 'flipped' in any way.

As you can see, this means there's only one correct solution to the Cube – when every one of those 26 cubies is in the correct position – and

43,252,003,274,489,856,000

ways the Cube can be scrambled. If you stacked that many standard-sized Cubes into a tower, it would reach an astonishing 274 light-years away.

Now that we know how the Cube is put together, we need to learn a few more terms before we can explain how to solve it . . .

THE FACES

As we solve the Cube, we will need to keep track of which face is which.

UP FACE
Hold the Cube with the white centre piece on top. We will call that face the **Up** face.

DOWN FACE
The opposite face (with the yellow centre piece) will be – you guessed it – the **Down** face.

FRONT FACE
Whichever face is facing you, we'll call **Front**.

BACK FACE
The opposite face will, of course, be the **Back**!

↓

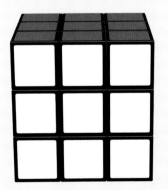

As you solve the Cube, you'll be turning it round in your hands from time to time. If the white face is the Up face and you turn over the Cube, the yellow face will now be the Up face. When you're following the instructions, keep holding the Cube the same way until you're told to turn it over or turn it round – otherwise, you will get in to all kinds of trouble.

LEFT FACE

The face to the left of the Front face is the **Left** face . . .

RIGHT FACE

. . . and the face to the right is the **Right** face. Simple!

INDIVIDUAL CUBIES

At certain points when solving the Cube you will need to pay attention to particular positions – often, the **front-top-right corner**. That is, looking at the Front face of the Cube, the cubie in the top right corner.

All the methods in this book depend on holding the Cube correctly, so if you're having trouble check that it's the right way round.

FRONT-TOP-RIGHT CORNER

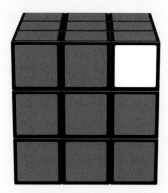

THE TURNS

These instructions are going to use what are known as **algorithms**. An algorithm is just a sequence of instructions, telling you which faces to turn in which directions in which order. We will use a standard notation for the turns, which you can see over the next few pages. The ones you will use most often are **U, D, B, F, L and R, and are all clockwise turns.**

U

Turn the Up face
clockwise

D

Turn the Down
face clockwise

B

Turn the Back
face clockwise

When we say 'clockwise', imagine you are looking **directly at that face's centre cubie.** If you are looking at the Front face, **U** means you turn the Up face to the right; **D** means you turn the Down face to the left. **Try these out to get used to them.** It takes a little practice to remember which direction to turn them and if you turn a face the wrong way the algorithm will fail to work properly. We will also want to turn faces **anticlockwise.** To show that, we will put a little apostrophe after the letter: so if the algorithm wants you to turn the Up face anticlockwise, it will say **U'.**

Turn the Front
face clockwise

Turn the Left
face clockwise

Turn the Right
face clockwise

OTHER NOTATION

Sometimes in the algorithms you will see the number 2 after a letter – **R2**, for example. This just means do the move twice – so **R2** means two turns.

You will also sometimes see brackets, like (**R U R' U'**) (**R U R' U'**). This doesn't change how you do the moves – it's just to group commonly-used little sequences of moves together to make them easier to learn.

ADVANCED TURNS

We've learned the turns you'll need most often, but there are some extra ones which will mainly show up in the advanced method (from page 56).

DOUBLE LAYER TURNS

Here you need to turn two layers at once. We use lower-case letters for these, and turn the layers the same way as you would for the single layer version. The **u** turn means turning the top two layers clockwise, for example. In this book we use **u**, **l** and **d**, but **f**, **b** and **r** work the same way.

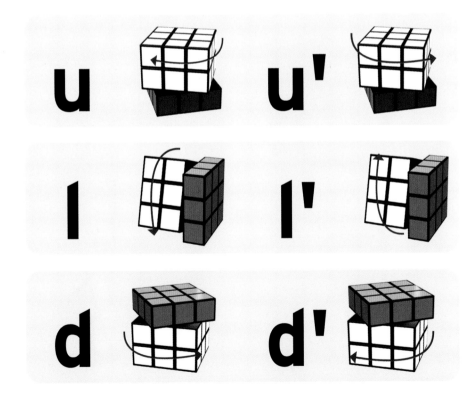

SLICE TURNS

The **slice** turns are applied to layers sandwiched between two other layers. These can be a little tricky to pull off quickly, as you will need to hold the two outer layers in place. The ones we will use later in this book are **M** and **E** – the other slice layer is called **S**.

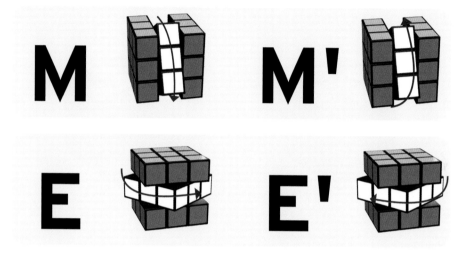

ROTATIONS

Sometimes we will want to turn the whole Cube in our hands. In this book, we will use the **X** and **Y rotations**. (See if you can work out what **Z** does!)

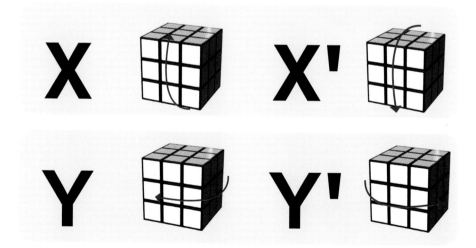

THE BEGINNERS' METHOD

Now that we've learned the turns, the faces and the notation, it's time to solve the Cube using the beginners' method. We'll do it one layer at a time – first we will solve the white face, then the middle layer, then the yellow face.

We will do the white edge pieces first . . .

then the white corner pieces . . .

then the edge pieces in the middle layer . . .

then the yellow edges . . .

and finally the yellow corners.

You don't have to start with the white face if you don't want to – you can choose any face, and the algorithms will work the same way. If you're trying to speed-solve the Cube, start with the face whose edge pieces look the easiest to solve. But if this is your first time, start with the white face, as then the diagrams in this book will all match what you're seeing.

DON'T PANIC!

Most importantly: if you go wrong, **don't panic**! The most common reasons would be that you have turned a face the wrong way, or turned the Cube around in your hand. See if you can retrace your steps, or just start again. The more you get used to this method the fewer mistakes you will make. If you forget what direction to turn a face in, there's a quick-reference at the bottom of each page.

THE WHITE CROSS

The first thing we need to do is to make a **white cross**. Turn your Cube so that the **white centre piece** is on top. We now need to move each of the four white edge pieces – white/orange, white/blue, white/green and white/red – to the top layer and put them in the correct places.

You can tell when they are in the right place because they will match with the orange, blue, green and red centre pieces as shown:

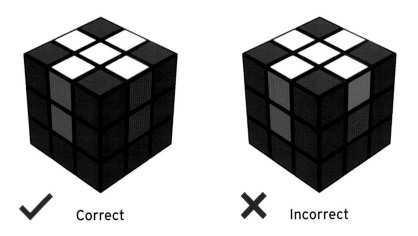

✔ Correct   ✗ Incorrect

There are lots of ways to do this depending on where the edge pieces are to begin with. They could be in the top layer, the middle layer, or the bottom layer. That's why this step is usually done intuitively, rather than by following algorithms; but there are a few tips to get you started.

> Don't panic! This is the hardest step to explain, but you will soon get the hang of it. Once you've solved the White Cross, the rest is easy.

First, let's see if there's an easy one to solve: an edge piece in the top (white) layer. If there isn't, move one to the top by turning the appropriate face.

URNS   U   U'   D   D'   B   B'

If the white face is pointing upwards, just turn the top face until it's in the correct position.

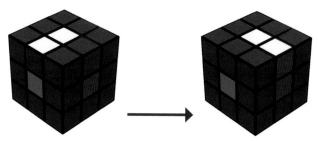

If the edge piece is in the top layer, but its white face is not pointing upwards, hold the Cube so that the cubie's white face is pointing to the right. Now do this:

R' F'

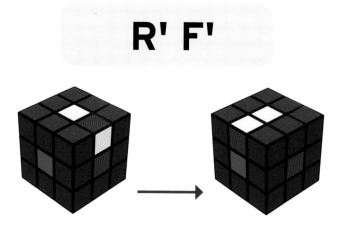

Now just turn the top layer until the edge piece is in the right place:

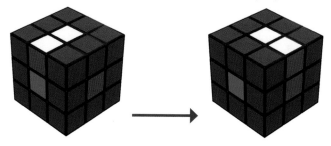

For the next three edges, we need to be careful not to mess up anything we've already solved. If they are in the top layer, you can use an **L2**, **R2**, **F2** or **B2** move to get them into the bottom later, which you can turn without worrying about messing up the top layer. They can then be moved into the correct position with another **L2**, **R2**, **F2** or **B2** move:

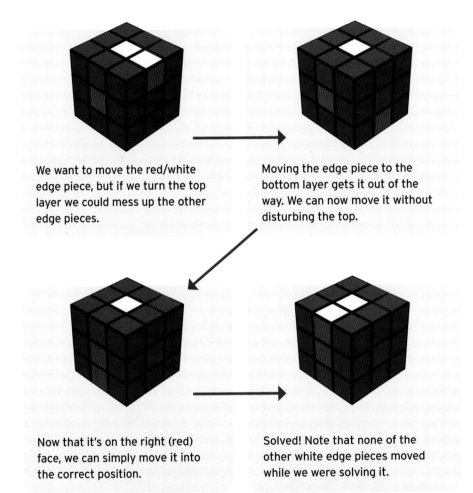

We want to move the red/white edge piece, but if we turn the top layer we could mess up the other edge pieces.

Moving the edge piece to the bottom layer gets it out of the way. We can now move it without disturbing the top.

Now that it's on the right (red) face, we can simply move it into the correct position.

Solved! Note that none of the other white edge pieces moved while we were solving it.

If they are in the middle layer, you can, again, move them into the bottom layer, rotate them to the correct face, and then back up to the top.

TURNS U U' D D' B B'

Sometimes you may find yourself in a situation where you have no choice but to move an edge piece you have already solved in order to solve another one. Keep track of it so that you can put it back at the first opportunity.

If you have an edge piece in the right position, but oriented the wrong way, here's how to fix it without messing up any of the other solved edges. This will move the solved white/green edge briefly, but put it back:

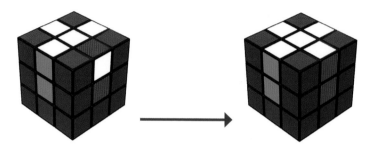

R' F D F' R2

When all the edges are in the right slots and oriented correctly, congratulations! You've done the hard part. Now to move on to the white corners . . .

> Once you have mastered the White Cross, practise solving it with the Cube upside-down – that is, with the yellow face pointing upwards. It's a little harder, because you can't see the face that you're solving, but if you are trying to solve the Cube quickly – for example, if you are using the Advanced method for speed-cubing (page 56) – it's faster.

THE WHITE CORNERS

There are four white corner pieces: **white/red/blue**; **white/green/red**; **white/blue/orange**; and **white/orange/green**. Below you can see the latter piece in the correct position and orientation. You can tell because the white, orange and green faces of the cubie are on the white, orange and green faces.

Look at the bottom layer. Find a white corner piece down there, and turn the Down face until the white corner cubie is **directly under** the spot where it's supposed to go. We will now do an algorithm which **moves** the cubie into the correct position and facing the right way.

If you were very unlucky, there aren't any white corner pieces in the bottom layer, and the ones in the top layer are in the wrong slots. Use one of these algorithms to swap them down to the bottom first.

Hold the Cube so that the cubie you want to move is in the **front-bottom-right** corner and the spot you want to move it to is in the **front-top-right** corner. We're going to move each white corner cubie in turn, moving each one from the front-bottom-right corner to the front-top-right corner.

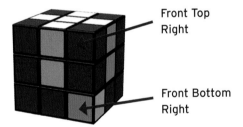

Front Top Right

Front Bottom Right

Look at which way the white face of the corner cubie is facing. It could be facing front, right or down. Depending on which direction it's facing, do one of the following algorithms:

FRONT: **F D F'**

RIGHT: R' D' R

DOWN: R' D D R D R' D' R

When you've successfully moved one of the corners, find the next corner piece and move it into position on the bottom layer. Turn the Cube in your hands so that the cubie is in the front-bottom-right position, directly below its correct slot, as before. Continue until all four corners are solved.

Again, if a white corner cubie is in the top layer, but in the wrong position, or facing the wrong way, just do any one of the above algorithms. It will move it down to the bottom layer, allowing you to then put it in the right slot using the appropriate algorithm.

If you've done this correctly, then the top layer of the Cube should now be completely solved.

Congratulations! That wasn't that difficult, was it?

THE MIDDLE LAYER

Turn your Cube over so that the white face is now the Down face and the yellow face is the Up face. The red, blue, green and orange faces should all have a solid line of the correct colour on the bottom layer.

We're now going to move the four middle-layer edge pieces into the right places. There are **four** edge pieces on the Up face. You need to find one that **doesn't** have any yellow on it, such as the **red/blue** edge piece or the **orange/green** edge piece. As you can see, these pieces need to move into the middle layer, and rotate 90 degrees. We will be swapping them with the cubie the arrow is pointing to.

Because we haven't started on solving the top layer yet, we can turn the Up face as much as we like without causing problems. Turn it so that the edge piece you're going to move completes an upside-down T shape of one colour on the Front face, as in the diagram below. As you can see, you'll need to move it down into the middle layer and either to the left or to the right, so that it's between the correct faces. Here are the algorithms to do that:

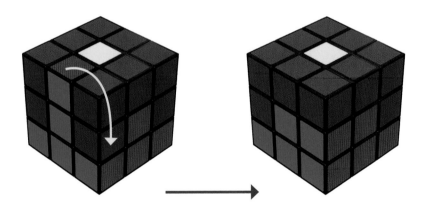

RIGHT: U R U' R' U' F' U F

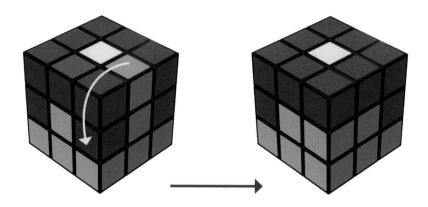

> If you end up with (or start with) an edge piece in the right position, but it is facing the wrong way, you can put one of the yellow edge pieces from the top layer in its place using one of these two algorithms. (It doesn't matter which yellow edge piece you use.) This will bring the edge piece you are interested in back up into the top layer, and you can now solve it as normal.

Use these algorithms to solve all four edge pieces and you have now solved the middle layer! The red, green orange and blue faces should now look like this:

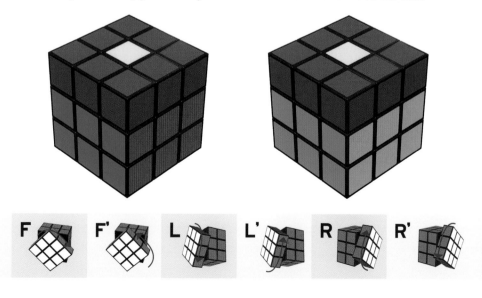

THE YELLOW CROSS

Now we need to make a **yellow cross** on the Up face. If you're lucky, you might already have got one by accident! If not, here's how to do it:

Look at the yellow face of the Cube. **Ignore the corners** and just look at the edge pieces. You will either have a **DOT**, an **L-SHAPE** or a **LINE**.

A DOT is just the centre piece, with no other yellow edge pieces facing upwards.

If you have a dot, hold the Cube any way you like.

An L-SHAPE is the centre piece with two other edge pieces facing upwards, making a right-angle.

If you have an L-shape, hold it so that the L-shape is in the top-left corner of the top face, like this:

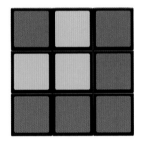

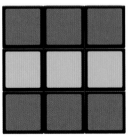

A LINE is the centre piece with two other edge pieces facing upwards, making . . . well, a line.

If you have a line, hold it so that the line goes horizontally across the top face, from left to right.

When you're holding it correctly, do this algorithm:

F R U R' U' F'

This algorithm turns dots into L-shapes, L-shapes into lines, and lines into crosses.

You can skip a step if you have the L-shape: you can just do this:

F U R U' R' F'

F  F'  L  L'  R  R'

THE YELLOW EDGES

You've got a yellow cross, but probably the edge pieces aren't in the correct positions. You now need to get them into the right places.

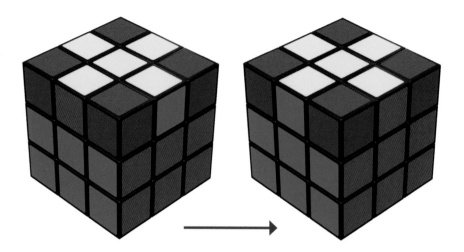

To do this, turn the Up face until you can see two adjacent edge pieces that, when swapped with each other, would be in the right slots. Hold the Cube so that one of them is facing you and the other is on the Left face. Then do this algorithm to swap them:

R U R' U R U U R' U

If you can't find two adjacent pieces to swap, you'll need to do this algorithm anyway, to move the edge pieces around.

THE YELLOW CORNERS

The yellow corner cubies are now all on the top layer, and we need to put them in their correct places. It doesn't matter if they are facing the wrong way, just that the yellow/green/red cubie is in the corner between the yellow, green and red faces, and so on.

Look at the top layer and see if you can find a yellow corner cubie that is in the right slot, even if it's oriented the wrong way.

No yellow corner cubies in the correct slots? Don't worry. Just do the below algorithm until there is at least one.

Hold the Cube so that the correct cubie is in the front-top-right slot. Then do this algorithm, which shuffles the other three corner cubies in the top layer:

U R U' L' U R' U' L

Check the Cube. Are all the corners in the right slots? If not, do it again until it looks right.

Remember, it doesn't matter if the cubies are facing the wrong way as long as they are in the right slots. We will flip them round in the next step.

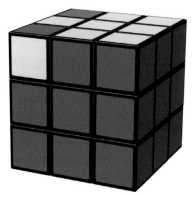

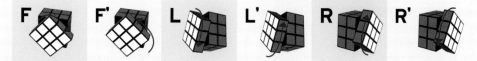

FINISHING THE CUBE

Now all we need to do is to re-orient any of the yellow corners which are facing the wrong way. We'll need to flip them so that the yellow face is pointing upwards. Find a corner that you need to re-orient, and hold the Cube so that it is in the **front-top-right corner.**

There are two very important things to note with this final step. First, when you do the next algorithm, it **will** mess up some of the parts of the Cube that we previously solved. **Don't panic!** It will fix itself before too long. Secondly, between steps, **don't turn the Cube in your hands**. Make sure the same face is facing you at all times.

So: you're holding the Cube so that the cubie you want to reorient is in the front-top-right corner.

Now do this:

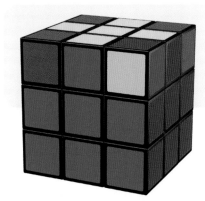

(R' D' R D)
(R' D' R D)

The brackets are there just to make it clear that it's the same algorithm twice in a row.

If the cubie isn't oriented the right way – with the yellow face pointing upwards – do that again. Each corner will need either two or four (**R' D' R D**) moves to fix.

Now that the corner cubie is facing upwards, you need to turn the Up face until another cubie that needs reorienting is in the front-top-right position. REMEMBER: **DON'T TURN THE WHOLE CUBE**. Just turn the Up face until another cubie that needs to be reoriented is in the front-top-right slot.

Here's an example of how your Cube might look after each corner is solved:

One solved

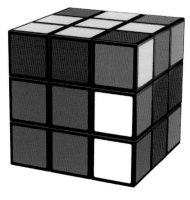

We've solved the cubie in the front-top-left position, and have turned the top face clockwise to bring another incorrectly-oriented cubie into the front-top-right slot for solving. As you can see, the Cube looks scrambled again, but it won't stay that way for long.

Two solved

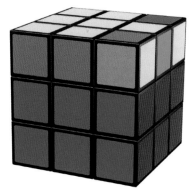

The next cubie is solved and we have brought another incorrect cubie into the front-top-right position. Note that the Cube's bottom two layers have unscrambled themselves!

Three solved

We've solved the third corner cubie, and again, the Cube looks scrambled. One more U move brings the last of the yellow corner cubies into position to solve. Remember: don't turn the Cube in your hands!

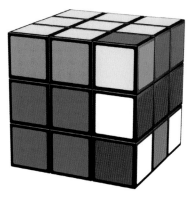

All solved

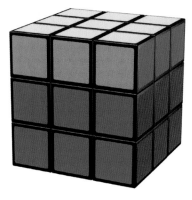

That's the last of the cubies oriented correctly and the bottom two layers have unscrambled themselves once more. Now all you need to do is to turn the top face . . .

And the Cube is solved! Well done!

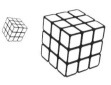

CONGRATULATIONS!

YOU SOLVED
THE CUBE!

PATTERNS

Now that you've solved the Rubik's Cube, why not try scrambling it in an interesting way next time? These algorithms will produce beautiful patterns:

CHECKERBOARD

U2 D2 F2 B2 L2 R2

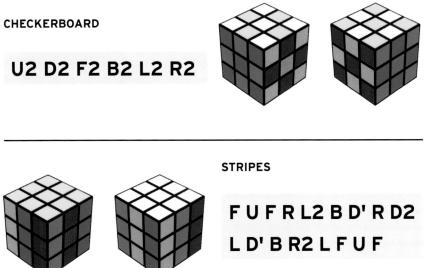

STRIPES

F U F R L2 B D' R D2
L D' B R2 L F U F

FLOWERS

U D' R L' F B' U D'

 U   U'   D   D'   B   B'

CROSSES

R2 L' D F2 R' D' R' L
U' D R D B2 R' U D2

ZIG-ZAGS

R L B F R L B F
R L B F

CUBE IN A CUBE

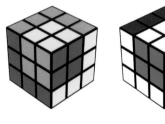

F L F U' R U F2 L2 U'
L' B D' B' L2 U

SUPERTWIST

F' U R' B' U' D L' F'
U R2 D F' L' U D' B'
R' D F'

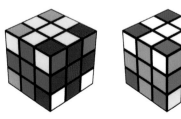

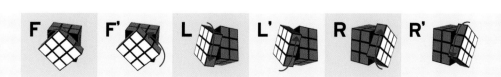

BUT CAN WE DO IT QUICKER?

Now you know how to do the Cube – but there are all kinds of challenges to try next. How fast can you do the Cube?

Speed-solving the Cube – speed-cubing – is a competitive sport. The Cube is scrambled, and the solver is allowed to study it; then, the clock starts ticking! At the time of going to press, the best time for the 3x3x3 Cube is an amazing 3.13 seconds, held by Max Park from the United States. (Check out the latest list of world records on pages 54–55!) To make solving the Cube even harder, expert speed-cubers also compete to solve them using only one hand, wearing a blindfold, or even with their feet!

To do the Cube this fast, you need a Cube that turns as easily and smoothly as possible. The standard Rubik's Cube is a marvel of engineering, but it isn't designed for super-quick solves. Rubik's make a special Speed Cube for this purpose, with special cores, highly-polished surfaces and adjustable internal springs. It's also a good idea to make sure that your speedcube is lubricated with a special gel.

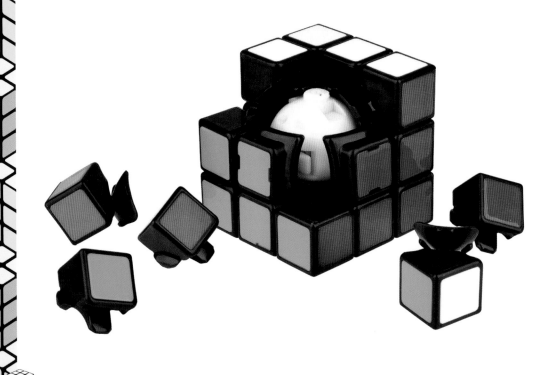

You will also need to solve the Cube in as few movements as possible. The method you have just learned is foolproof, but it's not as efficient as it could be – there are lots of ways to cut down the number of moves you will need. From page 56 we will learn a quicker method called **CFOP**.

The Cube has, for many years, fascinated mathematicians, and in 2010, using advanced maths and supercomputers, it was discovered that the maximum number of moves needed to solve a scrambled Cube is 20. This was a massive project which took weeks of computing time and examined trillions of possible cube positions.

If you want to try the hardest scramble that the researchers found, you can scramble your Cube like this:

F U' F2 D' B U R' F' L D'
R'U' L U B' D2 R' F U2 D2

WORLD RECORDS

At the time of going to print, these are the World Records for solving Rubik's puzzles!

THE 3x3x3 CUBE

Rank	Person	Result	Citizen of
1	Max Park	3.13	United States
2	Yusheng Du	3.47	China
3	Feliks Zemdegs	4.22	Australia
4	Feliks Zemdegs	4.59	Australia
	SeungBeom Cho	4.59	Republic of Korea

THE 2x2x2 CUBE

Rank	Person	Result	Citizen of
1	Guanbo Wang	0.47	China
2	Maciej Czapiewski	0.49	Poland
3	Rami Sbahi	0.58	United States
4	Christian Kaserer	0.69	Italy

THE 4x4x4 CUBE

Rank	Person	Result	Citizen of
1	Max Park	16.79	United States
2	Max Park	16.86	United States
3	Max Park	17.18	United States
4	Sebastian Weyer	17.42	Germany
5	Sebastian Weyer	18.25	Germany

THE 5x5x5 CUBE

Rank	Person	Result	Citizen of
1	Max Park	33.02	United States
2	Max Park	34.92	United States
3	Max Park	36.06	United States
4	Max Park	37.28	United States
5	Feliks Zemdegs	37.93	Australia

THE 3x3x3 CUBE - BLINDFOLDED

Rank	Person	Result	Citizen of
1	Tommy Cherry	12.78	United States
2	Tommy Cherry	12.97	United States
3	Tommy Cherry	14.51	United States
4	Tommy Cherry	14.61	United States
5	Tommy Cherry	14.67	United States

THE 4x4x4 CUBE - BLINDFOLDED

Rank	Person	Result	Citizen of
1	Stanley Chapel	51.96	United States
2	Stanley Chapel	57.87	United States
3	Stanley Chapel	1:02.51	United States
4	Stanley Chapel	1:06.23	United States
5	Stanley Chapel	1:06.84	United States

THE 5x5x5 CUBE - BLINDFOLDED

Rank	Person	Result	Citizen of
1	Hill Pong Yong Feng	2:19.07	Malaysia
2	Stanley Chapel	2:21.62	United States
3	Stanley Chapel	2:38.77	United States
4	Stanley Chapel	2:48.19	United States
5	Stanley Chapel	2:49.42	United States

THE 3x3x3 CUBE - ONE-HANDED

Rank	Person	Result	Citizen of
1	Max Park	6.20	United States
2	Max Park	6.82	United States
3	Feliks Zemdegs	6.88	Australia
4	Haixin Yang	8.27	China
5	Antoine Cantin	8.75	Canada

THE 3x3x3 CUBE - FEWEST MOVES

Rank	Person	Result	Citizen of
1	Sebastiano Tronto	16	Italy
2	Mark Boyanowski	17	United States
	Harry Savage	17	United Kingdom
4	Chad Batten	18	United States

THE CFOP METHOD

The **CFOP Method** is a way to solve the Cube in fewer movements – and hopefully less time – than the basic method you have now learned. It takes its name from:

Cross – First two layers – Orient last layer – Permute last layer

Rather than moving one cubie at a time, CFOP lets you move multiple cubies at once, so that you can solve the first two layers in four algorithms, and the last one with two. This is a lot more efficient than the basic method, and is the one used by most top speed-cubers.

1. THE WHITE CROSS

The first step – the White Cross – is the same as for the basic method, and is the step that relies most on your intuition. Try to do it with the white face on the bottom, rather than the top – it's important for speed solving, as you won't have to turn the Cube over. Remember, you don't have to start with the white cross if another cross is easier to make on a different coloured face.

2. FIRST TWO LAYERS

In this step we will solve the white corners in the bottom layer **and** the four edge pieces in the middle layer – and we can finish both those layers in four algorithms. Each time, we'll be moving a white corner piece **and** the edge piece that will sit directly above it – so, for example the white/blue/red corner piece and the blue/red edge piece will move together.

The tables on pages 58–59 show you which algorithm to use each time; you will need to pay close attention to the way your Cube looks in order to pick the right one. You may have to rotate the top (yellow) face in order to put the corner or edge pieces you want to move into a position that matches one from the table.

Corners that are in the wrong corner slots can be 'popped out' and into the top layer by moving the correct one in there – try to fix these first.

3. ORIENT LAST LAYER

Orienting the last layer means making all the yellow pieces face upwards - we don't mind if the cubies are not in the correct slots, just that they're all facing the right way. Here, you simply have to look at the top of the Cube and find the corresponding pattern in the tables on pages 60–62. Hold the Cube so that it looks **exactly like it does in the diagram**, then do the appropriate algorithm and we've finished this step.

4. PERMUTE LAST LATER

Permuting the last layer means shuffling the cubies so that they go into the correct slots, finishing the Cube. Here you will need to look at the table of algorithms on page 63. The arrows show which slots the cubies will move to and from; a line with an arrow on each end means the two cubies will swap places. You might need to turn the Cube round in your hands, looking at the top face, to see which diagram matches your Cube; or turn the whole top face until it matches a diagram.

Congratulations! You've solved the Cube using the advanced method! Now you just need to learn all those algorithms . . .

THE FIRST TWO LAYERS

There are 41 algorithms here – you need to find the one that corresponds to the corner and the edge pieces you're trying to move. Remember, you may need to turn the Up face to get the Cube looking like one of the cases in the table. For these algorithms, the blue face will be the Front face, and the red face will be the Right face.

Corner in bottom layer, edge in top layer:

 (U R U' R') (U' F' U F)

 (U' F' U F) (U R U' R')

 (F' U F) (U' F' U F)

 (R U R') (U' R U R')

 (R U' R') (U R U' R')

 (F' U' F) (U F' U' F)

Corner in bottom layer, edge in middle layer:

 (R U' R' d R' U2 R)
(U R' U2 R)

 (R U' R' U' R U R')
(U' R U2 R')

 (R U' R' U R U2 R')
(U R U' R')

 (R U' R' d R' U' R)
(U' R' U' R)

 (R U R' U' R U' R')
(U d R' U' R)

Corner in top layer, edge in middle layer:

 (R U R' U') (R U R' U')
(R U R')

 (R U' R') (d R' U R)

 (U F' U F) (U F' U2 F)

 (U F' U' F) (d' F U F')

 (U' R U' R') (U' R U2 R')

 (U' R U R') (d R' U' R)

Corner and edge in top layer, corner pointing right or front:

 R U R'

 F' U' F

 U' F' U F

U R U' R'

 (R U' R' U) (d R U' R)

(F' U F U') (d' F U F')

(U F' U2 F) (U F' U2 F)

(U' R U2 R') (U' R U2 R')

(U F' U' F) (U F' U2 F)

(U' R U R') (U' R U2 R')

(U' R U' R' U) (R U R')

(U F' U F U') (F' U' F)

(U' R U R' U) (R U R')

(U F' U' F U') (F' U' F)

(U F' U2 F U') (R U R')

(U' R U2 R' U) (F' U' F)

Corner and edge in top layer, corner pointing up:

(R U R' U') U' (R U R' U') (R U R')

Y' (R' U' R U) U (R' U' R U) (R' U' R)

(U2 R U R') (U R U' R')

(U2 F' U' F) (U' F' U F)

(U R U2 R') (U R U' R')

(U' F' U2 F) (U' F' U F)

 (R U2 R') (U' R U R')

(F' U2 F) (U F' U' F)

ORIENT LAST LAYER

Next we are going to flip all of the yellow pieces face-up. Here you just need to find the pattern that looks like the top of your Cube, and follow the algorithm. Make sure to hold your Cube so that the top face looks the same as in the table. The yellow lines show you which way the yellow faces of the cubies are pointing.

Dots:

 (R U2 R') (R' F R F') U2 (R' F R F')

 F (R U R' U') F' f (R U R' U') f'

 f (R U R' U') f' U' F (R U R' U') F'

 f (R U R' U') f' U F (R U R' U') F'

 (R U R' U) (R' F R F') U2 (R' F R F')

 M U (R U R' U') M2 (U R U' r')

 M U (R U R' U') M' (R' F R F')

 F (R U R' U) Y' R' U2 (R' F R F')

Lines:

 (R U R' U) R d' R U R' F'

 R U2 R2 (U' R U' R') U2 (F R F')

 f (R U R' U') (R U R' U') f'

 F (R U R' U') R F' (r U R' U') r'

Crosses:

 R U2 (R2' U' R2 U') (R2' U2 R)

 (R U R' U) (R U' R' U) (R U2 R')

 (R U2 R') U' (R U' R')

(R' U2 R) U (R' U R)

(r U R' U') (r' F R F')

R2 D (R' U2 R) D' (R' U2 R')

F' (r U R' U') (r' F R)

Corners:

 M' U' M U2' M' U' M

 (R U R' U') M' (U R U' r')

Squares:

 (R U2 R') (R' F R F')
(R U2 R')

 F R' F' R U R U' R'

r U2 R' U' R U' r'

 r' U2 (R U R' U) r

Small L Shapes:

(R' F R' F') R2 U2 Y
(R' F R F')

(I' U' L U') (L' U L U') L' U2 l

(r U R' U) (R U' R' U)
R U2' r'

R' F R2 B' R2' F' R2 B R'

F' (L' U' L U) (L' U' L U) F

F (R U R' U') (R U R' U') F'

(R U R' U) (R' F R F')
R U2 R'

(R U R' U') R' F R2 U R'
U' F'

S Shapes:

F (R U R' U') F' U F
(R U R' U') F'

r' U' R U' R' U2 r

(r U R' U) R U2 r'

F' (L' U' L U) F Y F
(R U R' U') F'

(L F' L' F) L' U2 L d (R U R')

(R U R' U) R U2 R' F
(R U R' U') F'

 (R U R' U') R U' R' F' U'
(F R U R')

(R' F R F') (R' F R F')
(R U R' U') (R U R')

C Shapes:

R' U' (R' F R F') U R

(R U R' U') X D' R' U R U' D X'

Big L Shapes:

(R' F R) U (R' F' R) Y' (R U' R')

F (U R U' R2) F' (R U R U' R')

l' U' l (L' U' L U) l' U l

r U r' (R U R' U') r U' r'

P Shapes:

f (R U R' U') f'

R' U' F U R U' R' F' R

F U R U' F' r U R' U' r'

f' (L' U' L U) f

T Shapes:

F (R U R' U') F'

(R U R' U') (R' F R F')

W Shapes:

(R U R' U) (R U' R' U') (R' F R F')

(L' U' L U') (L' U L U) (L F' L' F)

Z Shapes:

R' F (R U R' U') F' U R

L F' (L' U' L U) F U' L'

PERMUTE LAST LAYER

Now all the yellow pieces are facing upwards, but they probably aren't all in the right place. You can swap them around with the algorithms below – the lines show which cubies move to which positions. Find the algorithm that swaps or moves the correct pieces and you're done!

Ua: R2 U (R U R' U') (R' U') (R' U R')

Ub: (R U') (R U) (R U) (R U') R' U' R2

Z: M2 U M2 U M' U2 M2 U2 M' U2

H: M2 U M2 U2 M2 U M2

Aa: X ((R' U R') D2) ((R U' R') D2) R2

Ab: X' ((R U' R) D2) ((R' U R) D2) R2

E: X' (R U' R') D (R U R') u2 (R' U R) D (R' U' R)

Ga: R2 u R' U R' U' R u' R2 (Y' R' U R)

Gb: (R' U' R) Y R2 u R' U R U' R u' R2

Gc: R2 u' R U' R U R' u R2 (Y R U' R')

Gd: (R U R') Y' R2 u' R U' R' U R' u R2

F: (R' U2 R' d') (R' F') (R2 U' R' U) (R' F R U' F)

Ja: (R' U L') (U2 R U' R' U2) (R L U')

Jb: (R U R' F') (R U R' U') (R' F) (R2 U' R') U'

Na: (L U' R) U2 (L' U R') (L U' R) U2 (L' U R') U

Nb: (R' U L') U2 (R U' L) (R' U L') U2 (R U' L) U'

Ra: (L U2' L' U2') (L F') (L' U' L U) (L F) L2' U

Rb: (R' U2 R U2) (R' F) (R U R' U') (R' F') R2 U'

T: (R U R' U') (R' F) (R2 U' R') U' (R U R' F')

V: (R' U R' d') (R' F') (R2 U' R' U) (R' F R F)

Y: F R U' R' U' (R U R' F') (R U R' U') (R' F R F')

QUICK REFERENCE

Here are all the steps and algorithms you need for the beginner method.

1. The White Cross: Do this intuitively!

2. The White Corners: Hold the Cube so that the corner cubie you wish to move into the top layer is directly below its correct position. If the white face of the cubie is facing you, do this:

 FRONT: **F D F'**

If facing to the right, do this:

 RIGHT: **R' D' R**

If facing down, do this:

 DOWN:
R' D D R D R' D' R

Do this for all four corners. If one of the cubies is in the top layer already, but in the wrong place or facing the wrong way, swap another cubie into its place using the algorithms above so you can move it around the bottom layer.

3. The Middle Layer: To move an edge piece from the top to the correct position in the middle do this to move it left:

 LEFT:
U' L' U L U F U' F'

And this to move it right:

 RIGHT:
U R U' R' U' F' U F

4. The Yellow Cross: Hold the Cube as shown and perform the following algorithm. Repeat until the yellow cross appears.

F R U R' U' F'

5. The Yellow Edges: To swap adjacent edges, hold the Cube so that one is on the front face and one on the left face and do this:

 **R U R' U R U U R' U**

6. The Yellow Corners: To cycle the corners until they are in the correct positions, hold the Cube so that there is a correct cubie in the front-top-right position, then do this and repeat until correct.

 U R U' L' U R' U' L

7. Finishing the Cube: To flip the corners so that they are pointing the right way, hold the Cube so that the cubie you wish to reorient is in the front-top-right position, then do this either two or four times until fixed:

(R' D' R D) (R' D' R D)

Then turn the top face (**U** or **U'**) until the next cubie you wish to reorient is in this position. DO NOT TURN THE WHOLE CUBE, just the top face.